The New Evangelisation

What it is and how to do it

by
Fr Stephen Wang

All booklets are published thanks to the
generous support of the members of the
Catholic Truth Society

CATHOLIC TRUTH SOCIETY
PUBLISHERS TO THE HOLY SEE

Contents

All rights reserved. First published 2013 by The Incorporated Catholic Truth Society, 40-46 Harleyford Road London SE11 5AY Tel: 020 7640 0042 Fax: 020 7640 0046. © 2013 The Incorporated Catholic Truth Society.

ISBN 978 1 86082 887 4

Introduction

In 1983 Blessed Pope John Paul II spoke to the Catholic Bishops of Latin America in Haiti and called for a New Evangelisation: one that would be "new in its ardour, methods and expression". More recently, in 2010, Pope Benedict established a Pontifical Council for Promoting the New Evangelisation, to help the Church share "the inestimable gift" that God has given us, the gift of being "sharers in his own life". And when Pope Francis stepped onto the balcony of St Peter's Basilica for the first time on the day of his election it was significant that he spoke about his hopes for "the evangelisation of this beautiful city" - a city that many assumed had already been evangelised.

Evangelisation is not something new. Christians have been sharing their faith for two thousand years: giving witness to the love of God in Jesus Christ, and inviting others to share in that redeeming love through faith and the sacramental life of the Church.

Why, then, do we need a *New* Evangelisation? If the city of Rome has been a centre of Christian faith for many centuries, what does it mean for Pope Francis to say that it still needs evangelising?

To Bring Good News

First of all, we can make some straightforward distinctions. The word 'evangelisation' comes from a Greek verb that simply means 'to bring good news to others'. Anything that involves sharing the Christian faith and bringing others to know Christ and his Church is part of the work of evangelisation.

Primary evangelisation is understood to be the task of reaching out to those people and cultures that have never known Christ and his Gospel. It is 'missionary work' in its traditional sense, sometimes called the mission *ad gentes*, meaning 'to the (non-Christian) nations'. This is the first and in some senses the most important kind of evangelisation.

The *New Evangelisation*, according to Blessed John Paul II, concerns another situation. It involves the mission of the Church "particularly in countries with ancient Christian roots, and occasionally in the younger churches as well, where entire groups of the baptised have lost a living sense of the faith, or even no longer consider themselves members of the Church, and live a life far removed from Christ and his Gospel" (*Redemptoris Missio*, Para 33). The New Evangelisation, on this first definition, involves the re-evangelisation of former Christian cultures and of Christians who have become disconnected from their faith. Pope Benedict explains very simply that it is the need for a renewed missionary impulse in territories that have traditionally been Christian.

On the other hand, the distinctions between different kinds of evangelisation are not always so clean. The New Evangelisation is a cluster of ideas about mission and culture that are not easy to define. Greg Willets has written that defining the New Evangelisation "is like herding squirrels: it can take you in a multitude of different directions, sometimes all at once" (*CatholicDigest.com*). And even Pope Benedict, when he established the new Pontifical Council, admitted that this involves a variety of situations that demands careful discernment: "to speak of a 'new evangelisation' does not in fact mean that a single formula should be developed that would hold the same for all circumstances."

The Aims of this Booklet

This booklet recognises this variety and in Part 1 sets out five distinct but connected reasons why the Church needs to engage in an evangelisation that is truly new. In Part 2 it then presents a number of New Evangelisation 'projects' that have developed in the UK over the last few years. In Part 3 it draws out from these projects some consistent features of the New Evangelisation as it has been practiced effectively in the UK. Finally, in Part 4, the booklet collects together some of the most significant writings about the New Evangelisation from recent papal teaching and Church documents, as a resource for further reflection.

This booklet is not intended to be an introduction to the very idea of evangelisation: it takes for granted a basic understanding of why Christians want to share their faith and what this involves - theologically and pastorally; and it does not enter into the practical aspects of what individuals or parishes can do to evangelise. The intention here is very limited: to write about the distinctive features of the New Evangelisation, and to stimulate people to consider what this could mean for them and their communities.

Acknowledgements

Many of these ideas have been developed in other contexts. I'd like to thank Brother Mark O'Connor FMS for inviting me on behalf of the Archbishop's Office for Evangelisation to speak in the Archdiocese of Melbourne about the New Evangelisation in 2011; Fr Paul Mason for inviting me to speak to the clergy of the Archdiocese of Southwark about these topics in 2012; and the journal *The Tablet*, for allowing me to adapt some ideas that were first published there in an article entitled 'The New Evangelisation in Practice', 22nd January 2011.

I'd also like to thank the five groups mentioned in Part 2 for conversations about their work, and to acknowledge here my involvement with them in different capacities: as National Chaplain to Youth 2000, Chaplain to Catholic Voices, Theological Adviser to Ten Ten Theatre, one of the visiting lecturers for the SPES programme, and as a regular participant in the Spirit in the City festival.

Part 1: Five Reasons Why
We Need A New Evangelisation

Everyone has a slightly different explanation of why we need a New Evangelisation and exactly what the term means. These are the five reasons that come up most consistently in Catholic thinking. Taken together they form a kind of definition of what the New Evangelisation is and what its primary goals are.

(a) Living in a post-Christian society

Many countries that have historically identified themselves as Christian are now losing touch with their Christian roots. When this happens, the general culture often becomes increasingly secularised and pluralistic; the moral and legal assumptions of society are less and less influenced by Christian values; and fewer people identify themselves as Christian. There is, according to Pope Benedict, a "loss of the sense of the sacred" (*Ubicumque et Semper*).

This 'de-Christianisation' of society has been taking place for decades in most Western countries, especially within Europe, which has been at the heart of 'Christendom' for many centuries. It is also happening in places like Latin America, which has been a predominantly Christian continent for five hundred years.

This is not all negative. Some of the changes are to do with immigration and globalisation: societies are less homogenous and more pluralistic, which in many ways is a great gift. Some of the changes are to do with a greater social tolerance and a respect for difference and autonomy. But part of the situation is undoubtedly caused by an indifference to questions of faith, a lack of familiarity with the core Christian message, an increasingly materialistic outlook amongst many people, and sometimes an outright hostility to religion or to people of faith.

For some statistical evidence, here are some results from a recent census for England and Wales: "Between 2001 and 2011 there has been a decrease in people who identify as Christian (from 71.7 per cent to 59.3 per cent) and an increase in those reporting no religion (from 14.8 per cent to 25.1 per cent). There were increases in the other main religious group categories, with the number of Muslims increasing the most (from 3.0 per cent to 4.8 per cent)" (Office for National Statistics).

This isn't the first time that thriving Christian cultures have given way to a post-Christian landscape. By the fourth century, North Africa was predominantly Christian and home to some of the key figures of early Christian history, such as St Augustine of Hippo. Within a few centuries, these same territories were almost exclusively Muslim. And it took very little time for the communist regimes of Eastern Europe in the twentieth century to impose their atheistic ideologies on their citizens and drive religion, both Christian and non-Christian, almost completely underground.

Three Challenges

What, therefore, are the new challenges that our own 'post-Christian' situation presents for the task of evangelisation? There are three in particular:

First, many people in a post-Christian society believe that they already understand Christianity and are in a position to move beyond it. They believe that to some degree they have 'tried it' and found it wanting. In reality, they are often ignorant of the real meaning of Christianity, or they have never had it presented in an authentic and life-giving way. But this sense of their own familiarity can create a prejudice against Christianity, an assumed superiority, a lack of openness, that is absent in cultures that have never been influenced by the Christian message.

As Blessed John Paul wrote in *Ecclesia in Europa*, "Many Europeans today think they know what Christianity is, yet they do not really know it at all. Often they are lacking in knowledge of the most basic elements and notions of the faith" (Para 47).

Second, an aggressive secularism has developed in some of these Western countries that is much more than a benign post-Christian pluralism. Religion is dismissed out of hand by many people as something irrational and backward, or it is privatised and treated as an individual commitment that has nothing to do with public life or the common good. This attempt to create a neutral and even value-free public square ends up stifling debate and weakening society. It presumes that institutional religion has nothing to contribute to the common good, and forces individuals to separate themselves from their faith commitments if they have to deny their consciences when they participate in public roles (for example, as teachers, politicians, lawyers, doctors, etc.).

Third, despite the appearance of post-Christianity, many of these societies have deep Christian foundations that have not been completely undermined. The challenge is to rediscover the importance of these foundations, and to help people appreciate how much their culture has to gain from a greater understanding of its Christian roots. Christian history and Christian values, despite what many believe, are not a threat to a contemporary, pluralistic society, but a genuine help. As Pope Benedict said when he visited Westminster Hall in 2010, a society needs both faith and reason if it is going to root itself in objective moral principles.

Affirming Christian Values

When Pope Benedict spoke to the Queen in Edinburgh on the same UK visit, instead of criticising Britain for the process of de-Christianisation that seemed to be taking place, he sought to affirm the Christian values that were still very much a part of British culture. This recognition and reaffirmation are part of the New Evangelisation:

"The monarchs of England and Scotland have been Christians from very early times and include outstanding saints like Edward the Confessor and Margaret of Scotland. As you know, many of them consciously exercised their sovereign duty in the light of the Gospel, and in this way shaped the nation for good at the deepest level. As a result, the Christian message has been an integral part of the language, thought and culture of the peoples of these islands for more than a thousand years. Your forefathers' respect for truth and justice, for mercy and charity come to you from a faith that remains a mighty force for good in your kingdom, to the great benefit of Christians and non-Christians alike."

The New Evangelisation is trying to understand and speak to this broadly post-Christian society, with all its questions, dangers, possibilities and ambiguities.

(b) Christians disconnected from their faith

Another aspect of the contemporary situation, as mentioned in the Introduction, is that many people who call themselves Christian do not have a strong and life-giving faith.

Blessed John Paul II wrote about this in *Ecclesia in Europa*:

"Many of the baptised live as if Christ did not exist: the gestures and signs of faith are repeated, especially in devotional practices, but they fail to correspond to a real acceptance of the content of the faith and fidelity to the person of Jesus. The great certainties of the faith are being undermined in many people by a vague religiosity lacking real commitment; various forms of agnosticism and practical atheism are spreading and serve to widen the division between faith and life; some people have been affected by the spirit of an immanentist humanism [i.e. a view of the human person that has no room for faith and the transcendent], which has weakened the faith and often, tragically, led to its complete abandonment; one encounters a sort of secularist interpretation of Christian faith which is corrosive and accompanied by a deep crisis of conscience and of Christian moral practice" (Para 47).

There are many issues here, but the central point is that many baptised Christians do not have a living faith and a life-giving relationship with Jesus Christ their Saviour. This is not to judge or condemn anyone, or to expect that everyone's faith should be expressed in the same way; it's just to recognise - with sadness - that the Christian faith is skin deep for many people.

This is not a new situation historically. Many of the great missionary movements in seventeenth and eighteenth century Europe were founded to evangelise and catechise nominal Christians in Catholic countries who had had almost no Christian education or formation. This was especially true amongst both the rural and urban poor. But the fact that the situation has been a problem throughout Christian history does not make it any less worrying.

Catechised but not Evangelised

The normal pattern of Christian initiation is meant to run as follows (using the traditional theological language, and realising that this is a simplification): *initial proclamation; personal conversion; introductory catechesis; sacramental initiation; ongoing Christian formation; witness.*

Putting this into ordinary language: the basic message of Christianity is shared with someone ('proclamation'); this touches their heart and mind and leads them to take a step in faith and commit their lives to Jesus Christ ('conversion'); they then choose to learn more about this new faith, to grow into the Christian life, and to share more fully in the life of the Church ('catechesis'); this leads to the celebration of the sacraments and their wholehearted commitment to Christ and his Church ('sacramental initiation': Baptism, Confirmation and the Holy Eucharist); after this they continue to deepen their faith through their own efforts and with the support of the Church ('ongoing formation'); and they in their turn share the Christian faith with others through the example of their life and through their words ('witness').

In this pattern, *evangelisation* (the first two steps of proclamation and conversion) happens before *sacramental catechesis*. In other words, as a Christian is catechised and celebrates the sacraments, it is taken for granted that this person knows the basic message of Christianity and has taken this to heart, that they have a living faith, and that they have made a personal commitment to what they are learning and celebrating. The problem is that many Catholics, to use this technical language, are *catechised but not evangelised*; they are baptised and 'sacramentalised' but without having any real knowledge about what this means; they are nominally Catholic, culturally Catholic, but they lack a genuine conversion of heart and mind that would allow them to bring their Christian faith alive.

Catechesi Tradendae

In *Catechesi Tradendae* Blessed John Paul analyses the different reasons why this initial evangelisation has sometimes not taken place:

> "A certain number of children baptised in infancy come for catechesis in the parish without receiving any other initiation into the faith and still without any explicit personal attachment to Jesus Christ…In addition, there are other children who have not been baptised and whose parents agree only at a later date to religious education…Again, many pre-adolescents and adolescents who have been baptised and been given a systematic catechesis and the sacraments still remain hesitant for a long time about committing their whole lives to Jesus Christ…Finally, even adults are not safe from temptations to doubt or to abandon their faith,

especially as a result of their unbelieving surroundings. This means that 'catechesis' must often concern itself not only with nourishing and teaching the faith, but also with arousing it unceasingly with the help of grace, with opening the heart, with converting, and with preparing total adherence to Jesus Christ on the part of those who are still on the threshold of faith." (Para 19)

This, therefore, is one of the key challenges of the New Evangelisation: to help those Christians who are still "on the threshold of faith" to make a deeper commitment and discover the true riches of Jesus Christ; to call people to a genuine conversion even though they may already identify in some way as being Christian.

(c) New Culture, New Media

Another reason why we need a New Evangelisation is that the cultural situation has radically changed over the last two generations or so, particularly through globalisation and the development of new media. It was Blessed John Paul II's wish in 1983 that the Church would develop an evangelisation that was "new in its ardour, methods and expression".

One of the key reasons why we need new methods and modes of expression is because advances in information technology and digital media have utterly transformed the ways that human beings think and communicate. We could almost say that they have transformed the nature of what it is to be human, at least in terms of our understanding of ourselves and our relationships.

There have been similar social transformations in earlier Christian history: for example, the invention of the movable type printing press, the industrial revolution and the consequent urbanisation of society, the development of radio and television, etc. At each moment the Church has had to respond creatively and develop a new means of evangelisation appropriate to the situation. But perhaps no previous transformation has taken place so quickly and with such wide ranging effects as the digital communications revolution.

Pope Benedict's Reflections

Pope Benedict, apart from his decision to open a papal Twitter account, was not a pioneer in the area of new media and evangelisation. But his letters on the occasion of World Communications Day each year offer some of the most profound reflections on the New Evangelisation and the new media.

In 2009 he wrote about "the fundamental shifts in patterns of communication and human relationships" brought by the new digital technologies. He encouraged young people of the digital generation to use these technologies for good, in order to foster dialogue, connectedness and authentic friendship. Above all, he challenged them to be evangelists.

"The proclamation of Christ in the world of new technologies requires a profound knowledge of this world if the technologies are to serve our mission adequately. It falls, in particular, to young people, who have an almost spontaneous affinity for the new means of communication, to take on the responsibility for the evangelisation of this 'digital continent'. Be sure to announce the Gospel to your contemporaries with enthusiasm. You know their fears and their hopes, their aspirations and their disappointments: the greatest gift you can give to them is to share with them the 'Good News' of a God who became man, who suffered, died and rose again to save all people."

In 2010 Pope Benedict called on priests in particular to enter into the digital arena.

"The world of digital communication, with its almost limitless expressive capacity, makes us appreciate all the more Saint Paul's exclamation: 'Woe to me if I do not preach the Gospel!' (*1 Co* 9:16)...Priests stand at the threshold of a new era: as new technologies create deeper forms of relationship across greater distances, they are called to respond pastorally by putting the media ever more effectively at the service of the Word...Priests can rightly be expected to be present in the world of digital communications as faithful witnesses to the Gospel, exercising their proper role as leaders of communities which increasingly express themselves with the different 'voices' provided by the digital marketplace."

And in 2011 he went even further in highlighting the extraordinary newness of this new situation:

"I would like then to invite Christians, confidently and with an informed and responsible creativity, to join the network of relationships which the digital era has made possible. This is not simply to satisfy the desire to be present, but because this network is an integral part of human life. The web is contributing to the development of new and more complex intellectual and spiritual horizons, new forms of shared awareness. In this field too we are called to proclaim our faith that Christ is God, the Saviour of humanity and of history, the one in whom all things find their fulfilment (cf. *Ep* 1:10)."

A central part of the New Evangelisation is responding to this invitation to find ways of proclaiming Jesus Christ to others within this new digital world, and to discover what forms Christian faith may take in this radically new situation.

(d) Confusion about the need for evangelisation

One of the reasons why the New Evangelisation *feels* new, even though in this respect it isn't really, is because it represents a recommitment to the task of evangelisation after a period of theological confusion and crisis. In the period immediately after the Second Vatican Council, from the mid-1960s onwards, many Catholics came to believe that it was no longer necessary to proclaim the Gospel to non-Christians. There were a variety of reasons for this, and it is worth exploring some of them.

Vatican II

In the documents of the Second Vatican Council (also known as 'Vatican II'; 1962-65) certain theological themes came to the fore that seemed to represent a break with previous thinking, when in fact they were a continuation or a development of ideas that were part of the Church's received faith. These included the idea that salvation is possible for those outside the visible confines of the Catholic Church; that seeds of truth and goodness can be found in non-Christian religious traditions; that God's grace can work invisibly in the hearts of those who do not explicitly know Christ; and that Christians should respect the freedom of conscience of all people, especially in the area of religion (cf. *Unitatis Redintegratio* 3; *Ad Gentes* 11; *Gaudium et Spes* 22; *Lumen Gentium* 16-17; *Dignitatis Humanae* 3).

These are wonderful truths, which make up one important part of the Christian vision. Taken in isolation, however, they could lead to any number of false conclusions: for example, that people can be saved without

Jesus Christ; that the Catholic Church does not play an essential part in God's plan of salvation; that there is no need to share the Christian message with those who belong to another religious tradition; that everyone with a kind heart will automatically go to heaven when they die; that the grace given through the sacraments is unimportant and unnecessary; or that there is no need to appeal to someone's conscience if they are already convinced about the path they are on. Not one of these conclusions is found in the teaching of Vatican II or warranted by the theology of Vatican II.

Many of these false conclusions entered the mainstream of Catholic consciousness, and affected especially the field of 'missiology' - the theology of mission and evangelisation. This created a crisis within missiology in the 1970s and 1980s such that many theologians and missionary congregations became unsure about whether evangelisation was still a necessary part of the Church's mission. There was a fundamental doubt in some people's minds about the importance of faith in Jesus Christ and baptism into the Catholic Church.

Vatican II, 50 Years On

In a 2012 conference at Leeds Trinity University entitled Vatican II, 50 Years On: *The New Evangelisation*, Gavin D'Costa spoke about the dangers of taking statements from Vatican II in isolation. He showed how for every text that points to the work of the Holy Spirit outside the Church or the sacraments, there is another text - usually following on its heels - about the continuing importance of explicit faith in Jesus Christ, repentance, the Church, the sacraments, mission, evangelisation, etc.

It's not about playing one text off against another; it's about seeing that the Council is often holding together two truths, that are not contradictory, and that are both vitally important. First, our need as Catholics to be open to God's work in people's lives outside the Church; and second, the continuing need to evangelise.

Again and again, within the teaching of Vatican II, we are reminded about the importance of evangelisation. In *Lumen Gentium* it says, "The Church has received this solemn mandate of Christ to proclaim the saving truth from the apostles and must carry it out to the very ends of the earth. Wherefore she makes the words of the Apostle her own: 'Woe to me, if I do not preach the Gospel!' (*1 Co* 9:16)" (Para 17). And in *Ad Gentes* we hear: "The Church has an obligation to proclaim the faith and salvation which comes from Christ" (Para 5).

One passage in particular from *Ad Gentes* holds together the two inseparable theological truths:

> "So, although in ways known to himself God can lead those who, through no fault of their own, are ignorant of the gospel to that faith without which it is impossible

to please him (*Heb* 11:6), the Church, nevertheless, still has the obligation and also the sacred right to evangelise. And so, today as always, missionary activity retains its full force and necessity" (Para 7).

Recommitment to Primary Evangelisation

Part of the New Evangelisation, therefore, has been the Church's recommitment to primary evangelisation, after a time of theological confusion and crisis. This recommitment is nowhere clearer than in Blessed John Paul II's Encyclical Letter *Redemptoris Missio*. In fact the very reason for writing the letter was to respond to the crisis in missiology, as Blessed John Paul acknowledged:

"As a result of the changes which have taken place in modern times and the spread of new theological ideas, some people wonder: Is missionary work among non-Christians still relevant? Has it not been replaced by inter-religious dialogue? ...Does not respect for conscience and for freedom exclude all efforts at conversion? Is it not possible to attain salvation in any religion? Why then should there be missionary activity?" (Para 4)

Blessed John Paul's answer is emphatic:

"But what moves me even more strongly to proclaim the urgency of missionary evangelisation is the fact that it is the primary service which the Church can render to every individual and to all humanity in the modern world, a world which has experienced marvellous achievements but which seems to have lost its sense of ultimate realities and of existence itself. 'Christ the Redeemer,' I wrote in my first encyclical, 'fully reveals man to himself...The person who wishes to understand himself thoroughly must draw near to Christ....The Redemption that took place through the cross has definitively restored to man his dignity and given back meaning to his life in the world.'" (Para 2)

(e) Questions about the nature of Christian witness

A final reason why the Church needs a new commitment to evangelisation is because there has been some ambiguity about the meaning of Christian witness over the last half century or so. Even for those who are very committed to the idea of sharing the faith, there has sometimes been a hesitation about the need to explicitly proclaim the Gospel. This is the question of the relationship between the *witness of life* and the *witness of words*; between *example* and *proclamation*.

Broadly speaking, there are two ways that we witness to our faith and allow it to touch the lives of others. First, there is the *witness of our Christian life*: how we live at each moment; the example we give in every aspect of our lives; the ways we love, forgive, pray, speak, work, serve, laugh, cry; especially the ways that we relate to others and to God.

The witness of our life 'speaks' to others; it tells them, in a way that words never could, what is most important to us, what our convictions and priorities and values are. It is often silent and unselfconscious. Many people have been converted by the quiet example of Christians they have come to know. As St James says, "By my works I will show you my faith" (*Jm* 2:18).

Second, there is the *explicit witness of words*: when we speak to others about our Christian faith, telling them about the love of Christ and the salvation he offers, and inviting them to know him through faith, repentance, prayer and the sacraments of the Church.

Now this explicit witness doesn't necessarily come straight away. There is a time and a place, and it takes great sensitivity and the help of the Holy Spirit to judge when to speak. But one aspect of Christian witness is helping others to know what we believe and why we believe it, and giving them the possibility of learning more and making this faith their own. A coherent witness always involves personal testimony and the proclamation of the Gospel, as well as example and the quiet witness of our lives.

This should all be uncontroversial. The difficulty is that in the period following the Second Vatican Council there was very often an emphasis on the witness of life, dialogue with non-Christians, collaboration in works for justice, etc. - these are hugely important things - but this sometimes came with a neglect of the element of proclamation. Sometimes it was assumed that proclamation was not necessary - because the witness of life would be sufficient, or because an explicit proclamation might seem patronising, offensive or triumphalistic. Or there was the feeling that proclamation could be left to a group of 'specialists' (priests, religious, lay missionaries, etc), and that ordinary lay people should concentrate solely on their own quiet example.

Heralds of the Faith

The Catholic Church's response to this question has been to re-state very clearly that every Christian is called to witness to their faith both through their example and through their words. Of course there may be an emphasis, at any given moment, on one aspect rather than the other. But the idea that you can completely separate the witness of life and the witness of words is quite alien to the Christian vision.

This was clarified by Pope Paul VI in his 1975 Apostolic Exhortation *Evangelii Nuntiandi*. He did not in any way diminish the importance of Christian example: "For the Church, the first means of evangelisation is the witness of an authentically Christian life". And he made famous an often-quoted phrase about the need for witnesses: "Modern man listens more willingly to witnesses than to teachers, and if he does listen to teachers, it is because they are witnesses" (Para 41). A wordless Christian witness "is already a silent proclamation of the Good News and a very powerful and effective one. Here we have an initial act of evangelisation" (Para 21).

But Paul VI meets head on this question about whether the witness of life alone is enough. He writes:

"Nevertheless this always remains insufficient, because even the finest witness will prove ineffective in the long run if it is not explained, justified - what Peter called always having 'your answer ready for people who ask you the reason for the hope that you all have' (*1 P* 3:15) - and made explicit by a clear and unequivocal proclamation of the Lord Jesus. The Good News proclaimed by the witness of life sooner or later has to be proclaimed by the word of life. There is no true evangelisation if the name, the teaching, the life, the promises, the kingdom and the mystery of Jesus of Nazareth, the Son of God are not proclaimed" (Para 22).

Nor is this duty to proclaim the Gospel reserved for specialists. Every Christian, in virtue of their baptism, has a prophetic vocation. Lay people, as the Second Vatican Council explained, have a particular call to become powerful "heralds of the faith" in the secular world, "if they unhesitatingly join the profession of faith to the life of faith". This task of evangelisation, "that is, the proclamation of Christ by word and the witness of their lives, acquires a special character and a particular effectiveness because it is accomplished in the ordinary circumstances of the world" (*Lumen Gentium*, Para 35).

Taken together, these five reasons behind the New Evangelisation create a situation that is unique in the history of the Church. There is a new cultural situation, a new set of internal and external challenges for the Church, and a new clarity about the meaning and purpose of evangelisation.

Part 2: Five Examples of the New Evangelisation

The first part of this booklet has been slightly abstract, looking at the needs of the contemporary situation and the theology of the New Evangelisation. In this second part the focus is on the New Evangelisation in practice. What does it actually look like on the ground?

There are many exceptional initiatives taking place throughout the world. Here are just five examples of pastoral projects from the UK that represent different aspects of the New Evangelisation. They have not been chosen because they are necessarily the most successful or well-known projects. They are not offered as models of good practice to be imitated. But they may provide some ideas, some inspiration and a stimulus for discussion. They also happen to be projects with which the author has had some involvement, so that the descriptions here are based on first-hand experience.

These five examples help to illustrate some of the themes that have been touched on in Part 1, and they will provide material for discussion in Part 3 about practical approaches to the New Evangelisation. There is no space to outline the precise history of each project. These summaries just give a flavour of their work.

For more information about each of these initiatives you can easily search online for their websites.

(a) St Patrick's Evangelisation School

The history of St Patrick's Evangelisation School (SPES) is explained on its website:

> "SPES was set up in 2002 by the parish priest of St Patrick's Church in Soho, London, England in response to Blessed John Paul II's call to form disciples for the New Evangelisation. It is a nine-month course forming young people in the Catholic Faith: academically, spiritually, in community and in outreach to those who are marginalised in our society. Over the years the school has developed and is now well established within the parish and further afield."

The particular inspiration behind the initiative was Blessed John Paul II's suggestion that every parish should be a School of Evangelisation and should form apostles for the new millennium. In other words, we can't just leave this work of preparing for the New Evangelisation to the diocese or the religious orders or the New Movements. Every parish should be a vibrant centre of formation; every parish, if possible, should take the risk of being a School of Evangelisation. In St Patrick's they took this call literally.

SPES has five specific aims - to give young people the opportunity:

- To deepen their understanding of God's vocation for them and to respond more generously to the needs of Church.

- To be formed in the spiritual life through the daily pattern of Holy Mass, Adoration, praying The Rosary and Divine Office, as well as spiritual direction, community life, a regular programme of retreats.

- To increase their understanding of the *Catechism of the Catholic Church* and their readiness to give an account of the hope that is in them.

- To provide outreach to the poor and marginalised so that they may know the privilege of touching the Body of Christ.

- To take part in street evangelisation and other missionary work on a regular basis.

Each year a new group of young people takes up residence in the SPES community. They live an intense community life together, pray for an hour each day before the Blessed Sacrament, serve food to the homeless, run a Samaritans-style prayer-line, and go into the streets every Friday night - in a not too salubrious area - to meet people, share their faith, and offer spiritual support to those who seek it.

And they study. Fifteen hours a week of philosophy, theology, spirituality and psychology, focussed on preparing for the Certificate in Studies in the *Catholic Catechism* from the Maryvale Institute. There is a profound conviction that the Catholic faith is a gift to be understood and shared.

The effect on the young people themselves is profound. They grow in their faith, in their human maturity, and in their desire to serve others in different ways. Very often they gain a clearer sense of their vocation, of whether they are called to marriage, priesthood or some form of consecrated life. And the effect on the wider parish is equally profound. Just having a core group of people involved in this School for Evangelisation results in the whole parish being energised and committed to the task of the New Evangelisation. A small seed grows into a huge tree that bears much fruit.

(b) Spirit in the City

London is blessed to have four Catholic churches in the heart of the West End, which is one of the main districts for tourism, office workers, entertainment and nightlife: Notre Dame de France (Our Lady of France) near Leicester Square, Corpus Christi in Covent Garden, Our Lady of the Assumption and St Gregory near Piccadilly Circus, and St Patrick's in Soho Square (where the SPES programme is based).

Despite their unique locations, the parish teams went through a period of soul searching that will be familiar to many Catholics involved in parish life. Why is it, they asked, that so many people in the vicinity seem unaware of the Catholic presence here? We have so much to offer people: the beauty of our churches, the help and support that comes from Christian community, and above all the gift of faith and the love of Jesus Christ. And many people in the city seem to be lost or hurt or searching for something deeper in their lives. How can we reach out and connect with the hundreds of thousands of people who work in the area or come to visit?

The answer was for them to step outside the comfort of their buildings and their parish routines, and step into the lives of the people around them. And the concrete way they chose to do this was through the Spirit in the City festival.

This is from their website:

"Spirit in the City is a celebration of Christian faith in the heart of London, hosted by the Catholic churches in the West End. The annual festival aims to share the Good News of Christianity, and welcomes people of all faiths, ages and walks of life in the middle of the entertainment district. It gives an opportunity to raise deeper questions about life.

"We are all searching for new ways to connect with God and others around us. The events feature live music, workshops, talks, opportunities for prayer, reflection and reconciliation.

"Spirit in the City was born as an initiative of the local churches in 2006, as a response to the desire to share something of the Catholic faith with visitors and the West End community. The festival takes place in June over four days."

A Sanctuary of Silence

A quarter of a million people pass through Leicester Square in central London every day. By some kind of miracle, the four Catholic parishes in the area received permission from Westminster City Council to take over the square for one day each year as part of the festival. This involves a stage with non-stop music and talks; a line of stalls promoting various Catholic charities, movements and religious orders; a series of workshops about every aspect of Christian faith; a team of street evangelists greeting people and handing out prayer cards; a makeshift confessional with a rota of priests; and a suitably dignified tent-cum-chapel with the Blessed Sacrament exposed for adoration and personal prayer. It is the strangest thing to come out of Burger King and kneel before the Lord in the centre of Leicester Square - a sanctuary of silence in the madness of the city.

An important part of the festival is the processions. One evening there is a procession behind an icon of Our Lady and the Holy Child through the streets of Soho. The next evening there is a procession of the Blessed Sacrament that winds its way through the theatre district around Leicester Square before arriving at Corpus Christi church in Covent Garden. Three or four hundred people join the processions each year, praying, singing, with some people handing out leaflets and prayer cards to those sitting outside the nearby restaurants and pubs. Every year there are stories of remarkable conversations taking place about faith and prayer, and many onlookers find themselves willingly but unexpectedly drawn into the church for a moment of prayer and worship.

So there are often wonderful and visible fruits; but the main point of the festival is simply to give witness to the Christian faith and to be more present in the secular space outside the confines of the parish.

(c) Youth 2000

The aim of Youth 2000 is "to draw young people into a personal relationship with Jesus Christ, lived at the heart of the Catholic church." It does this primarily through weekend prayer festivals and local prayer groups, which are run by and for young people. It has flourished in the UK for over twenty years, and there are now thriving groups in other countries including France, Germany, Ireland and the United States.

The explicit purpose of Youth 2000 events is the evangelisation of young people: reaching out to those who have never heard of Jesus Christ, or to nominal Catholics and other Christians who have never had a strong experience of faith or a solid Christian formation.

The method is to introduce young people to the essentials of the Christian faith: the Mass, devotion to Our Lady, Adoration of the Blessed Sacrament, clear Catholic teaching expressed in a way that is relevant to their lives, a love for the Word of God, the sacrament of Confession, silent prayer and meditation, workshops about vocation and how to live one's faith in the world, the example and testimonies of young Catholic leaders, and an experience of fellowship and community through discussion groups, meals and social time. And the music at the retreats, provided by an experienced team of young musicians and singers, is often a key draw for the young people.

In one sense, these are aspects of the Christian life that you would hope to find in every parish. In another sense, it's not surprising that you sometimes need to go to a retreat or a prayer group to find them in abundance.

A particular feature of a Youth 2000 weekend or prayer group is to centre the whole event on the exposed Blessed Sacrament. In this way Jesus Christ, in his sacramental presence, is at the very centre of all of the prayer and teaching, and his divine presence can touch people's lives in powerful and unexpected ways.

In some ways this approach feels quite new - there are not many contemporary Catholic events that involve Perpetual Adoration, and it might seem that young people without a strong faith would not be 'ready' to appreciate the significance of the Blessed Sacrament. But there are echoes of the traditional Forty Hours devotion, when parishes will have an extended period of Adoration that involves prayer, teaching and the celebration of the sacraments.

A Gateway

There is no doubt that the Youth 2000 'formula' works. When young people are enabled to encounter Christ and his Church, and given the opportunity to pray and believe, they very often respond. Many genuine and lasting conversions have taken place through Youth 2000; and many young people have deepened their faith or discovered their vocation through the experience of a retreat weekend or prayer group.

One of the priorities of Youth 2000 over the last few years has been to help young people to live their faith in the ordinary circumstances of their parishes, schools, colleges and workplaces. Youth 2000 insists that it is not a 'movement' (there is nothing that you can actually 'join'). It characterises itself rather as a 'gateway' that helps people enter into the everyday life of the Catholic Church. A weekend retreat is meant to lead you more fully into the life of your home parish or student chaplaincy, where you can discover the same faith and the same sacraments that you have discovered while you have been away.

(d) Catholic Voices

In the run-up to Pope Benedict's visit to the UK in 2010 there was a lot of media interest in the Catholic Church, some of it positive and some negative. A small group of lay people was concerned that the Catholic voice might not be well represented in the media. Very often Catholic guests on TV or radio programmes seemed out of their depth intellectually or ill at ease in the studio, or at odds with the Catholic Church's position on a particular issue. So this group decided to get together a team of speakers who would be willing to put the case for the Church in the public square, and who would be positive about the opportunities for working within the secular media. The team would be authoritative and faithful to Catholic teaching, but not an official organ of the Church's hierarchy. Catholic Voices was born.

The twenty-four young adults on the first Speakers' Training Programme were not experts in theology or communication. They were simply committed Catholics who loved their faith and relished the opportunity to present it in an open and positive way, without being confrontational or defensive, and without watering it down. They were also chosen because they were articulate, confident and brave enough to step into media situations that could be quite testing.

The programme had three elements: spiritual formation (prayer, reflection, the celebration of Mass, a monastic retreat); training in media skills (interview techniques, presentation skills, role play, studio experience); and intellectual preparation (analysing the topical issues, briefings from experts in a particular field, understanding the Catholic point of view, appreciating the secular objections). It focussed on the 'hot topics' of the moment, the 'neuralgic issues' that touched a contemporary nerve. The aim was to prepare a team who would be "media-friendly, studio-ready and ego-free".

One of the key skills for the speakers is learning to 'reframe' an issue: to understand the 'positive intention' that usually lies behind a particular criticism of the Catholic view, and then to frame the argument in a way that speaks to that positive intention. For example, many pro-euthanasia campaigners are concerned to alleviate human suffering, and they fear that the Catholic pro-life position is indifferent to the suffering of the terminally ill. So the Catholic Voices speaker will try to acknowledge the positive intentions in the pro-euthanasia position, but show how they are better achieved through palliative care and respect for life, especially when it is most vulnerable.

Faith in its Integrity

In that period of the Papal Visit in 2010 Catholic Voices appeared on over one hundred TV and radio programmes.

It was a huge success, and made a big impression on Catholics and secular broadcasters alike. Since then the Catholic Voices project has developed in a number of ways. A new group of UK speakers has been trained each year since 2010. The CV Comment blog provides a regular commentary on important news items. The Catholic Voices Academy has held regular meetings in central London to help people wrestle with the most important issues facing contemporary culture. There has been a high-profile involvement in the campaign to defend conjugal marriage.

A number of important works have been published, such as *How to Defend the Faith Without Raising Your Voice*, which presents the key topics that come up for Catholics when they face the media, and *Who Know Where They Stand: Catholic Voices and the Papal Visit to the UK*, which explains the development of the whole project. And the Catholic Voices approach has quickly spread around the world, with associated projects developing in many countries in Europe, the Americas and Australia.

Part of the inspiration for Catholic Voices was a passage from a lecture by Blessed John Henry Newman:

"I want a laity, not arrogant, not rash in speech, not disputatious, but men who know their religion, who enter into it, who know just where they stand, who know what they hold, and what they do not, who know their creed so well that they can give an account of it, who know so much of history that they can defend it. I want an intelligent, well-instructed laity… I wish you to enlarge your knowledge, to cultivate your reason, to get an insight into the relation of truth to truth, to learn to view things as they are, to understand how faith and reason stand to each other, what are the bases and principles of Catholicism" ('Lectures on the Present Position of Catholics in England', No.9).

The work of Catholic Voices does not usually involve an explicit proclamation of the Gospel. It is, nevertheless, one important aspect of the New Evangelisation, because it seeks to present the Catholic faith in its integrity in the public square, and to see the media (both old and new) as an opportunity and not a threat.

(e) Ten Ten Theatre

An experienced actor and scriptwriter, with a deep faith and a desire communicate the Catholic moral vision, wanted to use drama to engage young people and bring alive the Gospel.

Ten Ten Theatre started with a series of short plays for teenagers, based on the experiences of young people, that dealt with themes such as relationships, chastity, bullying, violence, pregnancy, abortion, etc. Each session involved a performance of the play, followed by a guided discussion with the audience to draw out the themes and implications of the drama.

These are powerful dramas addressing profound moral dilemmas in contemporary language. They are not, however, value-free. In each play one of the characters gains a hard-won insight into a spiritual value or a moral truth. The dramatic development of the insight is often very subtle, and the values articulated are not always explicit. But the theological vision promoted by each play comes from a Catholic understanding of the human person and in particular from Blessed John Paul II's 'Theology of the Body'. Blessed John Paul, of course, was an actor as a young man before he was a priest; he tried to use theatre as a way of keeping alive a Christian humanism in the face of terrible political and religious oppression.

Drama as Witness

Drama is one of the most basic forms of witness. It speaks to the heart and gut as well as to the head. It's a way of presenting the faith without preaching; of leading people forward without lecturing them; of letting people see for themselves - in the characters before them on the stage - what a powerful difference it can make when someone does what is right and lives by a set of authentic Christian values.

The underlying intention of Ten Ten is to evangelise contemporary culture by stepping out into a particular world (a school or prison or community centre) and speaking to people in a language that they understand. Ten Ten is communicating Catholic values, and in particular the message of the Gospel of Life, to people who might be very disconnected from the practice of their faith. The name 'Ten Ten' comes from a reference to Chapter 10, Verse 10 of St John's Gospel: "I have come so that you may have life, life to the full." Through all of its work, Ten Ten aims to help people to "live life to the full."

The work has grown since its beginnings in 2007. There is now a cycle of age-appropriate plays about Relationship Education for children from age five to sixteen. The teams now work with teachers and parents whenever they visit a school, as well as with the children. Various projects have been developed for parishes, confirmation programmes, community groups, young offenders' institutions, prisons and school missions. Educational resources have been published. A number of professional plays are in development or have been put on in central London, in a secular context, that deal with themes such as love, faithfulness, sacrifice, martyrdom, human trafficking, etc.

Matthew Pinto has expressed his appreciation for this work on their website:

"The evangelistic and catechetical approach of Ten Ten Theatre is clearly among the most effective that I have seen. The leaders of this important apostolate clearly 'get it', in that they have a great love for Jesus Christ and the Church, yet also know how to speak the language of the age. They know all too well that, at times, we need to be 'all things to all men for the sake of the Gospel', as St Paul tells us. They do this in a manner that is completely faithful to Catholic teaching, but by no means heavy-handed. I expect them to continue to yield great fruit as they carry out the Church's call for a new evangelisation."

Part 3: Five Essential Ingredients of the New Evangelisation

When you look at the slightly random examples of the New Evangelisation presented in Part 2, and when you take into account many other similar projects throughout the world, there are certain common threads in their approach to the New Evangelisation, certain themes that emerge. We can call these the 'essential ingredients' of the New Evangelisation. Here are five of them.

These are not in any way the essential ingredients of *evangelisation in general*, which is a much bigger topic. There are no specific headings here, for example, about the Holy Spirit, faith, prayer, the Catholic Church, the Sacraments, witness, conversion, repentance, etc. It's necessary to take these for granted, and there is no space here to give an overview of the theology of evangelisation in general. These are just distinctive aspects that come to the fore when we think about the *New* Evangelisation.

Nor is this is to suggest that in order to evangelise everyone needs to be involved in a specific 'project'. There are many, many different ways of sharing the faith with others, and many if not most of them take place in the ordinary circumstances of everyday life and relationships. But these 'ingredients' will very often be part of the experience of the New Evangelisation, whether it is through an individual Catholic quietly witnessing to their faith, or a specific organisation that is established to promote the New Evangelisation.

(a) Personal conviction

Each of the five projects in Part 2 has been driven forward by people who have a profound love for the Lord and his Church, and a desire to share their faith with others. There is no evangelisation without a desire to evangelise.

Many Catholics, of course, love their faith, but not everyone has a deep conviction that this faith is meant to be shared, that it is something too precious to keep hidden. As Blessed John Paul II noted, "In the Church's history, missionary drive has always been a sign of vitality, just as its lessening is a sign of a crisis of faith" (*Redemptoris Missio*, Para 2).

Why Bear Witness?

When you look in the Gospels, there are three main reasons that lead people to speak to others about Christ and what he has done for them.

One is *joy*: many of those who are healed by Jesus or who witness a healing rush around telling everyone what has happened; they simply can't contain themselves - they are so excited and overjoyed (e.g. the deaf man in Mark

7:31-37, "They were astounded beyond measure, saying, 'He has done everything well; he even makes the deaf to hear and the mute to speak'"; and the blind men in Matthew 9:27-31, "But they went away and spread the news about him throughout the district").

Another is *love*: when someone's life is touched by the Lord, they want to share this experience with those they love, so that they too may come to know the love of Christ (e.g. when Andrew goes in search of his brother Simon Peter in John 1:40-42, and says to him, "We have found the Messiah", and brings him to Jesus; and Levi the tax collector in Mark 2:13-17, who hosts a dinner so that his friends can meet Jesus).

A third reason why people speak about Christ to others is *obedience*. Even if it is not always at first a heartfelt personal desire for everyone, Jesus sometimes just commands people to speak about him (e.g. the Demoniac in Mark 5:1-20, who wants to remain with Jesus after his liberation, but is told: "Go home to your friends, and tell them how much the Lord has done for you, and what mercy he has shown you"; and the eleven disciples after the Resurrection in Matthew 28:16-20, who are told, even as some of them doubt: "Go therefore and make disciples of all nations, baptising them in the name of the Father and of the Son and of the Holy Spirit, and teaching them to obey everything that I have commanded you").

Joy, love and obedience. These are the factors that motivate people to commit themselves to the New Evangelisation.

But this can be in sharp contrast to the reticence still felt by many Catholics about the very idea of evangelisation. There can be different reasons for this, not all of them negative: a desire to witness unobtrusively through one's personal example; a respect for the presence of God in people of other faiths or of no faith; a fear of appearing triumphalistic, arrogant or judgemental.

But the reticence can also reflect a subtle relativism that sometimes casts its spell, persuading Catholics that all beliefs are equally true, or that all truths are equally important. Many people aren't convinced that evangelisation is "the primary service which the Church can render to every individual and to all humanity" (*Redemptoris Missio*, Para 2).

Heart Speaks Unto Heart

Personal conviction is an essential motivating factor in the work of the New Evangelisation. It is also part of the *content* of what is communicated to others: we speak not just about the truths of our faith but also about what they personally mean to us and how they have changed our lives. This has often been an informal part of conversations between Christians and their non-Christian neighbours and friends. Catholics have become more aware in recent years of the power of personal testimony in witnessing to the faith.

Few people today doubt the effectiveness of personal witness in touching people's hearts and minds, whether it's a testimony given during a parish mission, a heartfelt conversation with a friend, a two-minute interview posted on YouTube, or a team of young people speaking about their faith at a school retreat. This was one of Blessed John Henry Newman's themes: 'Heart speaks unto heart', and it was evident during much of Pope Benedict's visit to the UK. When Barry and Margaret Mizen, parents of the murdered schoolboy Jimmy, gave a testimony at the Hyde Park vigil, they moved many people to tears. Their personal faith said more than a thousand sermons about the virtues of hope and forgiveness, and the power of Christ's love.

Without a strong personal conviction about the importance of evangelisation, and a willingness to share our faith in a personal way, the New Evangelisation will never really move forward.

(b) Community

An emphasis on community runs through the New Evangelisation. The aim is not just to proclaim the message, but to invite people into a way of life, a new set of relationships, and to show the beauty of a community founded on the love of Christ. This is, ultimately, an experience of the Church.

This comes in different ways. For many young Catholics, travelling to World Youth Day, for example, is the first time that they have had an experience of the Church beyond their own small parish communities and their schools. It's a time when their faith has come alive as if they have been evangelised for the first time. This was true for many people when they joined the crowds to visit the relics of St Thérèse on a tour of Britain in 2009, or lined the streets to greet Pope Benedict during his UK visit in 2010. Mission builds community, and depends on it.

This is seen in each of the five examples of the New Evangelisation above. There are different kinds of community represented here: a residential evangelisation school; a cluster of city centre parishes; a group of young people brought together by their faith and their desire to evangelise their peers; a team of skilled communicators united by a shared vision and a common training programme; a small theatre company with a network of loyal supporters and friends.

In each case, the effectiveness of the mission arises from the sense of community and common purpose that is formed when people have a shared commitment to evangelisation. This is thoroughly biblical. Jesus formed a group of seventy-two disciples to go ahead of him to prepare the local towns and villages for his own arrival; and even then he sent them out in pairs and not alone

(*Lk* 10:1-12). The powerful witness and preaching at Pentecost came from a community of disciples and not from an individual (*Ac* 2).

Specialised Communities

The Church needs communities dedicated to the New Evangelisation. These communities support and strengthen people so that they can 'go out on mission', whatever form that takes. And this creates a virtuous circle where the communities themselves are supported and strengthened through the shared experiences of the members. The New Evangelisation is not for isolated individuals; it depends on the Church and builds up the Church.

For most people, of course, the first community of the New Evangelisation should be their local parish, centred on the celebration of the Holy Eucharist each Sunday. This is the community that is meant to nurture faith and send us out into the world to witness to Christ in daily life. But even in the most faithful and life-giving parish, there will still be the need for specialised communities-within-the-community that can focus on particular aspects of the New Evangelisation, whether it is reaching out to young people, to parents and families, to the poor, to people in particular professions, to the media, etc. Each of these 'ministries' requires particular skills and evangelistic tools. Just as there have traditionally been guilds for doctors, lawyers and tradespeople; and support groups for mothers, fathers, young people and the elderly; so it should not surprise us that many new initiatives are springing up to facilitate the New Evangelisation in particular areas.

(c) The Word of God and the teaching of the Church

The New Evangelisation has been associated with a reverence for the Word of God in Sacred Scripture and a faithfulness to the teaching of the Catholic Church in its integrity. A new generation of evangelically minded Catholics has turned to the Bible and Catholic teaching for wisdom, nourishment, inspiration and renewal.

Catholics have always known this intellectually: that God's life-giving revelation, his Holy Word, is passed on to us through Scripture and Tradition, and interpreted through the teaching of the Catholic Church. But in recent years, in very concrete ways, different communities have seen how Scripture and Catholic teaching can transform people's lives and be a catalyst for conversion and renewal.

A New Hearing of God's Word

In his Post-Synodal Apostolic Exhortation *Verbum Domini,* Pope Benedict emphasised the link between the New Evangelisation and meditation on Sacred Scripture:

> "Our own time, then, must be increasingly marked by a new hearing of God's word and a new evangelisation. Recovering the centrality of the divine word in the

Christian life leads us to appreciate anew the deepest meaning of the forceful appeal of Pope John Paul II: to pursue the *missio ad gentes* and vigorously to embark upon the new evangelisation, especially in those nations where the Gospel has been forgotten or meets with indifference as a result of widespread secularism. May the Holy Spirit awaken a hunger and thirst for the word of God, and raise up zealous heralds and witnesses of the Gospel" (Para 122).

The emphasis on clear Catholic teaching seems to be an essential aspect of the New Evangelisation in its practice. Those involved want to proclaim the basic message of Christianity, to explain the core teachings of the Scriptures and of the Church, and to apply these teachings to everyday life. They are not arrogant, or unaware of the nuances and disputed questions within Catholic thought; but they are more interested in helping people to understand the settled faith of the Church than in exploring the boundaries. Their experience is that people are actually longing to learn more.

There is a hunger for truth in contemporary society, and a desire in many Catholic circles to share it. The intention is not to proselytise, in the sense of targeting people from other religions, but it is certainly to share this Christian vision with anyone who is attracted by it.

A New Apologetics

There has been a reticence in some Catholic circles over the last half-century about presenting the Catholic faith in its integrity and in an unapologetic way. There have been internal battles about Catholic teaching and identity. Sometimes there has been a lack of confidence that the Catholic vision is actually good news to be shared, or a fear that it will be ignored, rejected or even ridiculed. More recently, however, different groups such as Catholic Voices have been developing a New Apologetics. They are not strident, but they have a new confidence that Catholic teaching really matters, that it has something to say to the culture, and that it can make a difference.

One example of how confident catechesis and the New Evangelisation are intrinsically linked can be seen in the establishment of the Pontifical Council for Promoting the New Evangelisation. One its formal tasks, according to *Ubicumque et Semper*, is "to promote the use of the *Catechism of the Catholic Church* as an essential and complete formulation of the content of the faith for the people of our time". It recognises that you can't share a faith that you don't know; that effective evangelisation depends on good catechesis. Blessed John Paul had predicted that the *Catechism* would "make a very important contribution to that work of renewing the whole life of the Church" (*Fidei Depositum*).

Porta Fidei

In *Porta Fidei*, Pope Benedict's Apostolic Letter of 2012 for the Year of Faith, we read about the importance of the *Catechism*:

> "In order to arrive at a systematic knowledge of the content of the faith, all can find in the *Catechism of the Catholic Church* a precious and indispensable tool… Here, in fact, we see the wealth of teaching that the Church has received, safeguarded and proposed in her two thousand years of history. From Sacred Scripture to the Fathers of the Church, from theological masters to the saints across the centuries, the *Catechism* provides a permanent record of the many ways in which the Church has meditated on the faith and made progress in doctrine so as to offer certitude to believers in their lives of faith."

This is not just an intellectual journey, but an opportunity to meet the living Christ: "On page after page, we find that what is presented here is no theory, but an encounter with a Person who lives within the Church" (Para 11).

(d) Liturgy and the sacraments

The sacramental emphasis of the New Evangelisation is counter-intuitive. If you are reaching out to people with little or no faith, it's not clear why you would want to introduce them into a liturgical experience they probably wouldn't understand.

There are three reasons why the sacraments often form an effective part of the work of the New Evangelisation. First, in the post-Christian context, many enquirers often have some kind of Catholic or other Christian background, and some have even had some catechetical formation. So there is often a latent understanding of the meaning of the sacraments, an unacknowledged appreciation of their place in the Christian life. To celebrate the sacraments, and to speak about them, can help to awaken a half-formed memory of their significance. If there is a flicker of faith, it is often associated with a liturgical experience from the past, and so a new encounter with the sacraments can sometimes fan that tiny flame into something more powerful.

Second, very often the New Evangelisation involves not just talking to people but inviting them into the lived experience of a community of faith. An enquirer is often taken to a prayer group, or a mission in a parish church, or a celebration of the Holy Eucharist with a particular evangelistic focus. The celebration of the liturgy, whether the Church's public liturgy or her popular devotions or something more para-liturgical, is both the context in which the faith is being proclaimed and the lived expression of what this faith is ultimately about. People are brought into a community of faith, into a celebration of faith, and this helps them to see what it means in the round, in the flesh, and not just as an idea. The liturgy is the source and summit of the Christian life, and for that reason it can provide a rich context for conversion - if someone is led into it with sensitivity and helped to understand it in appropriate ways.

Third, the fact that Jesus Christ is present in the liturgy and the sacraments, supremely in the Holy Eucharist, means that an encounter with the liturgy is an encounter with Christ himself. This is true even if someone has no faith and no consciousness of Christ's presence, because there is an objectivity about his presence, even if it is hidden in the sacramental forms. This doesn't mean that someone should be dragged unwillingly before the sacraments as if there was some kind of guarantee that they would have a personal encounter with Christ. But if someone is open to the Christian faith, and freely chooses to come to the liturgy with an open heart and mind, this can create an opportunity for them to meet Christ in the sacraments and reach out to him in faith (but without encouraging them to participate sacramentally in a way that is inappropriate, because they are spiritually or catechetically unprepared).

The Source and Summit of Faith

It is an undeniable fact of Christian history that many people have been converted through an encounter with Christ in the liturgy, even though you might assume that their lack of faith would make their presence at the liturgy nonsensical. He speaks to them through the beauty of the liturgical celebration, or through the witness of the

Christian faithful, or through the proclamation of the Word of God, or through the sacramental presence of Christ himself, or through the holiness of the building - and in many other ways.

This is a common experience on youth retreats, even when they are aimed at non-Christians or nominal Catholics who have ceased practicing their faith. An example is the Youth 2000 prayer festival that takes place each year over the August bank holiday. Over a thousand young people flock to a field outside Walsingham, many of them with little or no commitment to the Christian faith. The Blessed Sacrament is exposed in the centre of the main tent for the whole duration of the festival, and at any moment a dozen priests are sitting round the edges of the tent to hear confessions. People are encouraged to pray, and to offer their lives to Christ in faith.

This living encounter with Christ in the Blessed Sacrament, even for those whose faith is just beginning, is very often the occasion of genuine Christian conversion and a source of life-changing graces. Many of the confessions have an almost baptismal quality about them, because it is often the first time that someone has really had the encouragement and the desire to bring their whole life to the Lord, without reservation. The sacraments, in much of the New Evangelisation, are the source and not just the summit of faith.

(e) Courage and creativity

Now and then, we are longing to share our faith, and a happy opportunity presents itself when we can speak with confidence and enthusiasm to someone who wants to listen to us. But more often than not, it's not clear what we should do or say, our faith is weak, our motivations are very mixed, and we are simply too nervous or afraid or unsure to take the next step.

It's difficult to evangelise. It's also one of the most important responsibilities that we have, and one of the most powerful ways in which God wishes to bless us. Faith is strengthened when we share it. Yet we often fail to share it because we think our own faith is not strong enough, when in fact our faith would become stronger if only we would share it more willingly.

Each one of the New Evangelisation initiatives described in Part 2 of this booklet took great courage and commitment to begin. Someone had an idea, or a quiet inspiration from the Holy Spirit, and they almost certainly thought to themselves, "I can't do this. It's too risky. I'm not ready. I don't have the support I need. It probably won't work." Yet they took the risk. They dared to do something different - with the help of God - and to do it with all the energy and creativity that they could muster.

Every Christian is called to take the risk of evangelising. We don't all have to go out into the streets and witness to strangers. But we do all have a responsibility to witness to our faith in everyday life, and to share our faith with others when the opportunity occurs.

Stepping Outside Ourselves

Pope Francis has spoken about the need for Catholics to take risks as they reach out to others. In an address to the ecclesial movements on the Vigil of Pentecost he said:

"At this time of crisis we cannot be concerned solely with ourselves, withdrawing into loneliness, discouragement and a sense of powerlessness in the face of problems. Please do not withdraw into yourselves! This is a danger: we lock ourselves up in our parish, among our friends, in our movement, with people who think as we do... but do you know what happens? When the Church is closed, she becomes an ailing Church, she falls sick. Think of a room that has been closed for a year. When you go into it there is a smell of damp, many things are wrong with it. A Church closed in on herself is the same, a sick Church.

"The Church must step outside herself. To go where? To the outskirts of existence, whatever they may be, but she must step out. Jesus tells us: 'Go into all the world! Go! Preach! Bear witness to the Gospel!' (cf. *Mk* 16:15). But what happens if we step outside ourselves? The same as can happen to anyone who comes out of the house and onto the street: an accident. But I tell you, I far prefer a Church that has had a few accidents to a Church that has fallen sick from being closed."

And in his Pentecost homily on the following day Pope Francis spoke about 'newness' in a way that can very easily be applied to the New Evangelisation:

"Newness always makes us a bit fearful, because we feel more secure if we have everything under control, if we are the ones who build, programme and plan our lives in accordance with our own ideas, our own comfort, our own preferences. This is also the case when it comes to God. Often we follow him, we accept him, but only up to a certain point. It is hard to abandon ourselves to him with complete trust, allowing the Holy Spirit to be the soul and guide of our lives in our every decision. We fear that God may force us to strike out on new paths and leave behind our all too narrow, closed and selfish horizons in order to become open to his own.

"Yet throughout the history of salvation, whenever God reveals himself, he brings newness and change, and demands our complete trust: Noah, mocked by all, builds an ark and is saved; Abram leaves his land with only a promise in hand; Moses stands up to the might of Pharaoh and leads his people to freedom; the apostles, huddled fearfully in the Upper Room, go forth with courage to proclaim the Gospel.

"This is not a question of novelty for novelty's sake, the search for something new to relieve our boredom, as is so often the case in our own day. The newness which God brings into our life is something that actually brings fulfilment, that gives true joy, true serenity, because God loves us and desires only our good. Let us ask ourselves: Are we open to God's surprises? Or are we closed and fearful before the newness of the Holy Spirit? Do we have the courage to strike out along the new paths which God's newness sets before us, or do we resist, barricaded in transient structures which have lost their capacity for openness to what is new?"

This is God's call to every Christian: to step out, to take the risk of doing something new and creative in order to spread the Gospel. Whether it is in a large and well-known project, or in the quiet circumstances of everyday life and work, each one of us is called to share our faith and take part in the New Evangelisation.

Part 4: Five Key Documents about the New Evangelisation

These texts are printed here so that readers can see how Catholic reflection has developed in the area of the New Evangelisation, and how the central ideas about the New Evangelisation have been expressed in papal teaching. Some of the writing is very theologically dense, but it will certainly repay careful study and meditation. This section forms a sort of compendium of recent Catholic teaching in these areas, and a resource for ongoing study.

Even though the term 'New Evangelisation' had not been coined when Pope Paul VI wrote *Evangelii Nuntiandi* in 1975, sections from this encyclical have been included because they are so important for the theology of the New Evangelisation.

The full texts of each of these documents can be found very easily by searching online.

(a) Pope Paul VI, *Evangelii Nuntiandi* (1975)

"The presentation of the Gospel message is not an optional contribution for the Church. It is the duty incumbent on her by the command of the Lord Jesus, so that people can believe and be saved. This message is indeed necessary. It is unique. It cannot be replaced…It is a question of people's salvation. It is the beauty of the Revelation that it represents. It brings with it a wisdom that is not of this world. It is able to stir up by itself faith - faith that rests on the power of God. It is truth. It merits having the apostle consecrate to it all his time and all his energies, and to sacrifice for it, if necessary, his own life" (Para 5).

"The Church…has a vivid awareness of the fact that the Saviour's words, 'I must proclaim the Good News of the kingdom of God,' apply in all truth to herself: She willingly adds with St Paul: 'Not that I boast of preaching the gospel, since it is a duty that has been laid on me; I should be punished if I did not preach it.' It is with joy and consolation that at the end of the great Assembly of 1974 we heard these illuminating words: 'We wish to confirm once more that the task of evangelising all people constitutes the essential mission of the Church.' It is a task and mission which the vast and profound changes of present-day society make all the more urgent. Evangelising is in fact the grace and vocation proper to the Church, her deepest identity. She exists in order to evangelise, that is to say, in order to preach and teach, to be the channel of the gift of grace, to reconcile sinners with God, and to perpetuate Christ's sacrifice in the Mass, which is the memorial of His death and glorious resurrection" (Para 14).

The Drama of Our Time

"The split between the Gospel and culture is without a doubt the drama of our time, just as it was of other times. Therefore every effort must be made to ensure a full evangelisation of culture, or more correctly of cultures. They have to be regenerated by an encounter with the Gospel. But this encounter will not take place if the Gospel is not proclaimed" (Para 20).

"Above all the Gospel must be proclaimed by witness. Take a Christian or a handful of Christians who, in the midst of their own community, show their capacity for understanding and acceptance, their sharing of life and destiny with other people, their solidarity with the efforts of all for whatever is noble and good. Let us suppose that, in addition, they radiate in an altogether simple and unaffected way their faith in values that go beyond current values, and their hope in something that is not seen and that one would not dare to imagine. Through this wordless witness these Christians stir up irresistible questions in the hearts of those who see how they live: Why are they like this? Why do they live in this way? What or who is it that inspires them? Why are they in our midst? Such a witness is already a silent proclamation of the Good News and a very powerful and effective one. Here we have an initial act of evangelisation…Other questions will arise, deeper and more demanding ones, questions evoked by this witness which involves presence, sharing, solidarity, and which is an essential element, and generally the first one, in evangelisation.' All Christians are called to this witness, and in this way they can be real evangelisers. We are thinking especially of the responsibility incumbent on immigrants in the country that receives them" (Para 21).

"Nevertheless this always remains insufficient, because even the finest witness will prove ineffective in the long run if it is not explained, justified - what Peter called always having 'your answer ready for people who ask you the reason for the hope that you all have' - and made explicit by a clear and unequivocal proclamation of the Lord Jesus. The Good News proclaimed by the witness of life sooner or later has to be proclaimed by the word of life. There is no true evangelisation if the name, the teaching, the life, the promises, the kingdom and the mystery of Jesus of Nazareth, the Son of God are not proclaimed" (Para 22).

The Living Witness of the Church

"Without repeating everything that we have already mentioned, it is appropriate first of all to emphasise the following point: for the Church, the first means of evangelisation is the witness of an authentically Christian life, given over to God in a communion that nothing should destroy and at the same time given to one's neighbour with limitless zeal. As we said recently to a group of lay people, 'Modern man listens more willingly to witnesses than to teachers, and if he does listen to teachers, it is because they are witnesses.' St Peter expressed this well when he held up the example of a reverent and chaste life that wins over even without a word those who refuse to obey the word. It is therefore primarily by her conduct and by her life that the Church will evangelise the world, in other words, by her living witness of fidelity to the Lord Jesus - the witness of poverty and detachment, of freedom in the face of the powers of this world, in short, the witness of sanctity" (Para 41).

(b) Blessed Pope John Paul II, *Redemptoris Missio* (1990)

"I wish to invite the Church to renew her missionary commitment. The present document has as its goal an interior renewal of faith and Christian life. For missionary activity renews the Church, revitalises faith and Christian identity, and offers fresh enthusiasm and new incentive. Faith is strengthened when it is given to others! It is in commitment to the Church's universal mission that the new evangelisation of Christian peoples will find inspiration and support.

"But what moves me even more strongly to proclaim the urgency of missionary evangelisation is the fact that it is the primary service which the Church can render to every individual and to all humanity in the modern world, a world which has experienced marvellous achievements but which seems to have lost its sense of ultimate realities and of existence itself" (Para 2).

"God is opening before the Church the horizons of a humanity more fully prepared for the sowing of the Gospel. I sense that the moment has come to commit all of the Church's energies to a new evangelisation and to the mission *ad gentes*. No believer in Christ, no institution of the Church can avoid this supreme duty: to proclaim Christ to all peoples" (Para 3).

Why Mission?

"To the question, 'why mission?' we reply with the Church's faith and experience that true liberation consists in opening oneself to the love of Christ. In him, and only in him, are we set free from all alienation and doubt, from slavery to the power of sin and death. Christ is truly 'our peace' (*Ep* 2:14); 'the love of Christ impels us' (*2 Co* 5:14), giving meaning and joy to our life. Mission is an issue of faith, an accurate indicator of our faith in Christ and his love for us.

"The temptation today is to reduce Christianity to merely human wisdom, a pseudo-science of well-being. In our heavily secularised world a 'gradual secularisation of salvation' has taken place, so that people strive for the good of man, but man who is truncated, reduced to his merely horizontal dimension. We know, however, that Jesus came to bring integral salvation, one which embraces the whole person and all mankind, and opens up the wondrous prospect of divine filiation…Newness of life in him is the 'Good News' for men and women of every age: all are called to it and destined for it.

"This is why the Church's mission derives not only from the Lord's mandate but also from the profound demands of God's life within us. Those who are incorporated in the Catholic Church ought to sense their privilege and for that very reason their greater obligation of bearing witness to the faith and to the Christian life as a service to their brothers and sisters and as a fitting response to God. They should be ever mindful that 'they owe their distinguished status not to their own merits but to Christ's special grace; and if they fail to respond to this grace in thought, word and deed, not only will they not be saved, they will be judged more severely' [*Lumen Gentium* 14]" (Para 11).

The Witness Par Excellence

"People today put more trust in witnesses than in teachers, in experience than in teaching, and in life and action than in theories. The witness of a Christian life is the first and irreplaceable form of mission: Christ, whose mission we continue, is the 'witness' *par excellence* (*Rv* 1:5; 3:14) and the model of all Christian witness. The Holy Spirit accompanies the Church along her way and associates her with the witness he gives to Christ (cf. *Jn* 15:26-27).

"The first form of witness is the very life of the missionary, of the Christian family, and of the ecclesial community, which reveal a new way of living. The missionary who, despite all his or her human limitations and defects, lives a simple life, taking Christ as the model, is a sign of God and of transcendent realities. But everyone in the Church, striving to imitate the Divine Master, can and must bear this kind of witness; in many cases it is the only possible way of being a missionary" (Para 42).

"Proclamation is the permanent priority of mission. The Church cannot elude Christ's explicit mandate, nor deprive men and women of the 'Good News' about their being loved and saved by God. 'Evangelisation will always contain - as the foundation, centre and at the same time the summit of its dynamism - a clear proclamation that, in Jesus Christ…salvation is offered to all people, as a gift of God's grace and mercy.' All forms of missionary activity are directed to this proclamation…

"The subject of proclamation is Christ who was crucified, died and is risen: through him is accomplished our full and authentic liberation from evil, sin and death; through him God bestows 'new life' that is divine and eternal. This is the 'Good News' which changes man and his history, and which all peoples have a right to hear. This proclamation is to be made within the context of the lives of the individuals and peoples who receive it. It is to be made with an attitude of love and esteem toward those who hear it, in language which is practical and adapted to the situation. In this proclamation the Spirit is at work and establishes a communion between the missionary and his hearers, a communion which is possible inasmuch as both enter into communion with God the Father through Christ" (Para 44).

(c) Blessed Pope John Paul II, *Ecclesia in Europa* (2003)

"In various parts of Europe a first proclamation of the Gospel is needed: the number of the unbaptised is growing, both because of the significant presence of immigrants of other religions and because children born into families of Christian tradition have not received Baptism, either as a result of the Communist domination or the spread of religious indifference. Indeed, Europe is now one of those traditionally Christian places which, in addition to a new evangelisation, require in some cases a first evangelisation.

"The Church cannot shirk the responsibility of making a courageous diagnosis which will make it possible to decide on appropriate therapies. On the 'old' continent too, there are vast social and cultural areas which stand in need of a true *missio ad gentes*" (Para 46).

"Everywhere, then, a renewed proclamation is needed even for those already baptised. Many Europeans today think they know what Christianity is, yet they do not really know it at all. Often they are lacking in knowledge of the most basic elements and notions of the faith. Many of the baptised live as if Christ did not exist: the gestures and signs of faith are repeated, especially in devotional practices, but they fail to correspond to a real acceptance of the content of the faith and fidelity to the person of Jesus. The great certainties of the faith are being undermined in many people by a vague religiosity lacking real commitment; various forms of agnosticism and practical atheism are spreading and serve to widen the division between faith and life; some people have been affected by the spirit of an immanentist humanism, which has weakened the faith and often, tragically, led to its complete abandonment; one encounters a sort of secularist interpretation of Christian faith which is corrosive and accompanied by a deep crisis of conscience and of Christian moral practice. The great values which amply inspired European culture have been separated from the Gospel, thus losing their very soul and paving the way for any number of aberrations.

Will He Find Faith on Earth?

"'When the Son of man comes, will he find faith on earth?' (*Lk* 18:8). Will he find faith in our countries, in this Europe of ancient Christian tradition? This is an open question which clearly reveals the depth and the drama of one of the most serious challenges which our Churches are called to face. It can be said as the Synod emphasised that this challenge frequently consists not so much in baptising new converts as in enabling those already baptised to be converted to Christ and his Gospel: in our communities we need to be seriously concerned about bringing the Gospel of hope to all those who are far from the faith or who have abandoned the practice of Christianity" (Para 47).

"Proclaiming the Gospel of hope calls for steadfast fidelity to the Gospel itself. The Church's preaching, in all its forms, must be increasingly centred on the person of Jesus and increasingly converge on him. Vigilant care must be taken that Christ is presented in his fullness: not merely as an ethical model, but above all as the Son of God, the one, necessary Saviour of all, who lives and is at work in his Church. If our hope is to be true and unshakable, 'an integral, clear and renewed preaching of the Risen Christ, the resurrection and eternal life' must be a priority for pastoral activity in coming years" (Para 48).

(d) Pope Benedict XVI, *Ubicumque et Semper* (2010)
[Establishing the Pontifical Council
for Promoting the New Evangelisation]

"It is the duty of the Church to proclaim always and everywhere the Gospel of Jesus Christ. He, the first and supreme evangeliser, commanded the Apostles on the day of his Ascension to the Father: 'Go therefore and make disciples of all nations, baptising them in the name of the Father and of the Son and of the Holy Spirit, teaching them to observe all that I have commanded you' (*Mt* 28:19-20). Faithful to this mandate, the Church - a people chosen by God to declare his wonderful deeds (cf. *1 P* 2:9) - ever since she received the gift of the Holy Spirit on the day of Pentecost (cf. *Ac* 2:14), has never tired of making known to the whole world the beauty of the Gospel as she preaches Jesus Christ, true God and true man, the same 'yesterday and today and for ever' (*Heb* 13:8), who, by his death and Resurrection, brought us salvation and fulfilled the promise made of old. Hence the mission of evangelisation, a continuation of the work desired by the Lord Jesus, is necessary for the Church: it cannot be overlooked; it is an expression of her very nature.

"In the course of history, this mission has taken on new forms and employed new strategies according to different places, situations, and historical periods. In our own time, it has been particularly challenged by an abandonment of the faith - a phenomenon progressively more manifest in societies and cultures which for centuries seemed to be permeated by the Gospel... There has been a troubling loss of the sense of the sacred, which has even called into question foundations once deemed unshakeable such as faith in a provident creator God, the revelation of Jesus Christ as the one Saviour, and a common understanding of basic human experiences: i.e., birth, death, life in a family, and reference to a natural moral law.

"Even though some consider these things a kind of liberation, there soon follows an awareness that an interior desert results whenever the human being, wishing to be the sole architect of his nature and destiny, finds himself deprived of that which is the very foundation of all things…

A Tragic Situation

"It is enough to recall what was affirmed [by Blessed John Paul] in the Post-Synodal Apostolic Exhortation *Christifideles Laici*: 'Whole countries and nations where religion and the Christian life were formerly flourishing and capable of fostering a viable and working community of faith, are now put to a hard test, and in some cases, are even undergoing a radical transformation, as a result of a constant spreading of an indifference to religion, of secularism and atheism. This particularly concerns countries and nations of the so-called First World, in which economic well-being and consumerism, even if coexistent with a tragic situation of poverty and misery, inspires and sustains a life lived "as if God did not exist". This indifference to religion and the practice of religion devoid of true meaning in the face of life's very serious problems, are not less worrying and upsetting when compared with declared atheism. Sometimes the Christian faith as well, while maintaining some of the externals of its tradition and rituals, tends to be separated from those moments of human existence which have the most significance, such as, birth, suffering and death [...].

"'On the other hand, in other regions or nations many vital traditions of piety and popular forms of Christian religion are still conserved; but today this moral and spiritual patrimony runs the risk of being dispersed under the impact of a multiplicity of processes, including secularisation and the spread of sects. Only a re-evangelisation can assure the growth of a clear and deep faith, and serve to make these traditions a force for authentic freedom.

"'Without doubt a mending of the Christian fabric of society is urgently needed in all parts of the world. But for this to come about what is needed is to first remake the Christian fabric of the ecclesial community itself present in these countries and nations' (n. 34).

"Making my own the concerns of my venerable Predecessors, I consider it opportune to offer appropriate responses so that the entire Church, allowing herself to be regenerated by the power of the Holy Spirit, may present herself to the contemporary world with a missionary impulse in order to promote the new evangelisation. Above all, this pertains to Churches of ancient origin, which live in different situations and have different needs, and therefore require different types of motivation for evangelisation...

Openness to the Gift of Grace

"This variety of situations demands careful discernment; to speak of a 'new evangelisation' does not in fact mean that a single formula should be developed that would hold the same for all circumstances. And yet it is not difficult to see that what all the Churches living in traditionally Christian territories need is a renewed missionary impulse, an expression of a new, generous openness to the gift of grace. Indeed we cannot forget that the first task will always be to make ourselves docile to the freely given action of the Spirit of the Risen One who accompanies all who are heralds of the Gospel and opens the hearts of those who listen. To proclaim fruitfully the Word of the Gospel one is first asked to have a profound experience of God.

"As I stated in my first Encyclical *Deus Caritas Est*: 'Being Christian is not the result of an ethical choice or a lofty idea, but the encounter with an event, a person, which gives life a new horizon and a decisive direction' (n. 1). Likewise, at the root of all evangelisation lies not a human plan of expansion, but rather the desire to share the inestimable gift that God has wished to give us, making us sharers in his own life."

(e) *Lineamenta* for the Synod of Bishops on the New Evangelisation (2011)

"Though well-known and undoubtedly a part of the Church's many projects, the 'new evangelisation' remains a relatively new expression and concept in ecclesial and pastoral circles. Consequently, its meaning is not always clear and precise. Initially introduced by Pope John Paul II during his apostolic visit to Poland, without any specific emphasis or idea of its future role, the 'new evangelisation' was used again and given new life in the Holy Father's Magisterium to the Churches in Latin America. Pope John Paul II used the term to reawaken and elicit renewed efforts in a new missionary and evangelising undertaking on the continent. In this regard, he said to the bishops in Latin America: 'The commemoration of this half millennium of evangelisation will have full significance if, as bishops, with your priests and faithful, you accept it as your commitment; a commitment not of re-evangelisation, but rather of a new evangelisation; new in its ardour, methods and expression.'

The Courage to Forge New Paths

"Consequently, the new evangelisation is not a matter of redoing something which has been inadequately done or has not achieved its purpose, as if the new activity were an implicit judgment on the failure of the first evangelisation. Nor is the new evangelisation taking up the first evangelisation again, or simply repeating the past. Instead, it is the courage to forge new paths in responding to the changing circumstances and conditions facing the Church in her call to proclaim and live the Gospel today. In the past, the Latin American continent was facing new challenges (the spread of a communist ideology, the appearance of the sects). The new evangelisation emerged after a process of discernment undertaken by the Church in Latin America to consider and evaluate the overall situation.

"In this sense, Pope John Paul II again took up the expression in his Magisterium and proposed it to the universal Church. 'Today the Church must face other challenges and push forward to new frontiers, both in the initial mission *ad gentes* and in the new evangelisation of those peoples who have already heard Christ proclaimed. Today all Christians, the particular Churches and the universal Church, are called to have the same courage that inspired the missionaries of the past, and the same readiness to listen to the voice of the Spirit.' The new evangelisation is primarily a spiritual activity capable of recapturing in our times the courage and forcefulness of the first Christians and the first missionaries. Consequently, it requires, first of all, a process of discerning the vitality of Christianity and a reconsideration of its accomplishments and the difficulties it has encountered. At a later date, Pope John Paul II clarified his idea of a new evangelisation: 'The Church today ought to take a giant step forward in her evangelisation effort, and enter into a new stage of history in her missionary dynamism. In a world where the lessening of distance makes the world increasingly smaller, the Church community ought to strengthen the bonds among its members, exchange vital energies and means, and commit itself as a group to a unique and common mission of proclaiming and living the Gospel. "So-called younger Churches have need of the strength of the older Churches and the older ones need the witness and impulse of the younger, so that individual Churches receive the riches of other Churches"'.

A Revitalised Church

"Presently, in reviewing the dynamics of the 'new evangelisation', the expression can now be applied to the Church's renewed efforts to meet the challenges which today's society and cultures, in view of the significant changes taking place, are posing to the Christian faith, its proclamation and its witness. In facing these challenges, the Church does not give up or retreat into herself; instead, she undertakes a project to revitalise herself. She makes the Person of Jesus Christ and a personal encounter with him central to her thinking, knowing that he will give his Spirit and provide the force to announce and proclaim the Gospel in new ways which can speak to today's cultures.

"Understood in this manner, the idea of a 'new evangelisation' was again taken up and proposed in the continental synodal assemblies, celebrated in preparation for the Jubilee of the Year 2000. At that time, it became an accepted expression in the pastoral and ecclesial thought of the local Churches. A 'new evangelisation' is synonymous with renewed spiritual efforts in the life of faith within the local Churches, starting with a process to discern the changes in various cultural and social settings and their impact on Christian life, to reread the memory of faith and to undertake new responsibilities and generate new energies to joyously and convincingly proclaim the Gospel of Jesus Christ. In this regard, the words of Pope John Paul II to the Church in Europe are particularly indicative and concise: '...an urgent need [has arisen] for a "new evangelisation", in the awareness that "Europe today must not simply appeal to its former Christian heritage: it needs to be able to decide about its future in conformity with the person and message of Jesus Christ"'" (Para 5).